FROM *Pain* TO POWER

An Intimate Reflection on the Journey to Self-Love

J'NITA

MELAN8T'D
PUBLISHING

FROM PAIN TO POWER
An Intimate Reflection on the Journey to Self-Love

Copyright © 2024 J'Nita

Published by Melan8t'd Publishing
Winston-Salem, NC

Printed in the United States of America
First Paperback Edition - June 2024

Paperback ISBN: 979-8-218-43174-7

Edited by: Khloe's Thoughts Editing
Cover by: Make Your Mark Publishing Solutions
Layout by: Make Your Mark Publishing Solutions

I dedicate this book to myself. Yes, I could dedicate it to the people who caused pain in my life to help me get to this point, but I am not giving them that power. I took back my power by turning the pain into something far beyond my imagination.

After reading this book, your new life motto should be "Healed and minding my peace."

Honor thy self.

~ *J'NITA*

Introduction

I wrote this book, as it was always my dream to write, but the genre was not the idea. Although I discuss turning Pain into Power, I am still on my journey to do so, and this is just the introduction to my story as well the story of others.

This book may seem incohesive, with random reflections, but that is how my self-love journey has been—all over the place. The journey to self-love and healing is not linear, as it has ups and downs and may have you in a whirlwind of emotions. So, the concept of this book is to allow yourself to go through those motions, to release the pain and turn it into something beautiful—your power of restoration.

Love is a topic heavily discussed these days, which many people struggle with— self-love, platonic, and intimate love. No one has the right answers to understand the intricate complexities of love, but many have a good understanding and advice. The reason there is no right answer to love is because it is an individualistic experience. My definition of love may be different from yours, your coworker, grandmother, parents, etc. It is not a one size fits all. So, when it comes to love, knowing what it means, looks like, and feels like is from your viewpoint. Knowing this allows you to only accept the love that meets your requirements and nothing less. Some people believe one should not start a new relationship when healing. Healing can take years, so if waiting is for you, then please take that time. If you have emotional and mental baggage, you should heal before bringing it into a relationship. Be honest with yourself and partner about your journey. Be with someone who is supportive of your healing, has patience, and provides a safe space to keep healing. Healing does not mean you will not desire love, intimacy, or companionship. It is natural to want and need, so do not deny yourself that opportunity.

Reflect

Have you ever been in a dark place in life? A place so dark you wanted to be surrounded by the darkness of evil. Not in the sense of being maleficent, but knowing you were protected and could defend yourself from people that aimed to harm you. This usually stems from pain very deep where it seems there is no light at the end of the tunnel. Due to not seeing any light, you may surround yourself in darkness as it may be comforting in your plight. Do not fret, there is light at the end, although you may have to endure the darkness to appreciate the light. Few, if anyone at all, knows us during our darkest moments. Hell, sometimes we do not even know ourselves during those troubling moments as some do not accept or confront it, so embrace it. Understand that being in your light is a form of protection. Your darkness may not be daggers struck into someone, death, or other harmful forms of protection, but a gentle redirection for you to change the direction of your life out of the negativity. Darkness may bring destruction for those with ill intent, but that is not for you to worry about. Being in light means you do not let the darkness of someone else invade your essence or energy. It means you continue to glow while darkness surrounds you. You are the light and only you can allow the darkness in, but if you choose to remain in the light, you will be protected by your peace. You will be protected by whoever and whatever source (God, ancestors, etc.) you believe in, even if you are your own source. It means you chose to live in your power of self-love. Love may be a difficult concept to embrace as many people have not experienced true love or self-love. Many of us have not had the love from family, friends, spouses, or even yourself. So, your journey may include learning to love yourself and the true meaning of love, which can illuminate the light at the end of the tunnel.

Reflect

_____

_____

_____

_____

_____

_____

_____

_____

_____

_____

_____

_____

_____

_____

_____

_____

Karma is not always "what comes around goes around." It brings things to light. Karma can be enlightenment, reflection, and insight of your thoughts, behaviors, patterns, and/or beliefs. This will make you sit in those uncomfortable truths/understanding of yourself and make you do a self-analysis. One may think, so what, I think about life/myself all the time. No, karma makes you wallow in self-analysis to the point of being uncomfortable with yourself. It makes you understand what needs to be changed and why. Karma is living a perpetual cycle of unfulfillment because you lack growth, wisdom, maturity, faith, self-love, and knowledge. Karma can be an emotional, mental, or even physical state of being that makes you feel trapped. Yes, it could manifest into the same things you have done to others, but your karma is about you. It can put you through emotional and mental turmoil that forces you to go within because at this point you have no control. You experience pain that no one else may be privy to. It inflicts you with so much grief you may need to rely on faith to get you out, yet you still need to do the work for your karma to be completed. If you choose to remain in an unhealthy or toxic way of being, karma will allow you to live in a state of hell with no peace of mind or success. Some people want to see the karma of those that did them wrong or have the comfort of knowing they will get what they deserve. Do not get caught up waiting for this to happen as it can become an obsession and you will be living in hell mad because you do not see justice being served. You give that person more power by giving your energy to them. Let them thrive and live their life, but one thing to remember is that we all put on an act in the public. Just because it does not look like karma is getting them, does not mean it is not. Again, everyone's karma, good or bad, is for that person to see and experience. It is your time now to turn your pain into power and live your life. A lot of people who have been hurt, regardless of the person or circumstances, may want to see justice served through karma. Is this because you feel karma has more power than you? Is it because you feel the wrong done to you was by someone who was/is more powerful? Karma may indeed have a power we are afraid to unleash or possess. The power of karma is the unknown, which makes it powerful. Think about the karma you had in your life. If you are someone that is very giving and help others, think about the good karma you received. I was a kind person (I learned it is not my job to help everyone, nor does everyone deserve my kindness) and was invested in helping others in need. Many of my good deeds were unreciprocated by those I helped. Even though I was not asking for anything in return, they did not return the favor when I needed help. Anyway, years/decades later when I was struggling financially and could not make ends meet, someone I was working with helped me out tremendously. I did not ask for their assistance, they just offered. They even declined when I wanted to return the favor. I learned this was my karma for the good I have done for others. To this day I am grateful for that individual. On the other hand, I have, too, received bad karma and learned my lessons from them. So, this is what I mean by the power of karma. It may not come immediately, but it will come— good or bad. For instance, karma has the power of breaking someone that is already broken, but not to the public's eye. Karma can delve into someone's insecurities, fears, or even wreak havoc on someone's dreams. This does not mean harming someone. You may feel weak and timid because you allowed someone into your life who caused you distress. You want to have victory and the power to release the pain, hurt, and anger, which you feel will be done by witnessing the karma. You know the saying "good things come to those that wait." Have you ever considered those that have done you wrong are waiting for their karma, but just do not know it. Karma is more patient than most of us could be. So, take control of your life and turn that pain into your power. Focus on yourself so you can live with peace. Living in peace and focusing on yourself can be in terms doing what is best for you. Living in peace can be manifested into your reality by living life that is righteously for you such as changing bad habits, speaking your mind, saying no, and reclaiming your happiness. It can mean no longer worrying about situations you cannot or should not be trying to control.

Reflect

_____

_____

_____

_____

_____

_____

_____

_____

_____

_____

_____

_____

_____

_____

_____

_____

_____

Lack of fulfillment in a relationship can be due to lack of value and substance within the dynamic (vice-versa). You need to be fulfilled in any relationship for it to thrive. This includes with yourself. If you do not nourish the relationship with yourself, you will look for that fulfillment in others and may experience disappointment as you neglect to foster the value and substance of your being. It is hard to want more from someone when you have only had a certain type of relationship with others for example sexual or unrequited love. Learning to accept and understand that you want more can be difficult when you have settled for less than you deserve and want. Being a confident, sensual, supportive, and loving partner, yet not reciprocating it can be challenging when you desire it from others. To manifest this into your life, you will have to change your mindset, perspective, behaviors, and choice of words. These changes are not an automatic guarantee it will come into fruition right away, but it changes how you perceive these types of relationships. It starts with you. It starts with loving yourself, believing in yourself, knowing your worth and value. It will not be easy because you need to work through your old belief system and behaviors, comfort zones, and be willing to put in the work to make the necessary changes. You will go through emotional, mental, and maybe even physical hardships to achieve what you want and desire. Self-love is key. The phrase "how can you love someone if you don't love yourself" is essential. It is essential because you need to know what love means to you, how you perceive, accept, and give love to yourself and others. It is essential because being ignorant to your needs, desires, and requirements will leave you repeating the same things and wandering aimlessly with no direction. Knowing how to embrace and give love is also essential. If you are greedy with love by only receiving and not giving, that can be difficult in your relationships with others. So, loving yourself provides you with the means to be properly loved and to properly love someone else. If you do not love yourself, how can someone else love you? How will they know how to love you, how will you know the type of love you expect, desire, and need? Not loving yourself can put you in a tricky situation, such as being with someone who does not know how to love or does not love themselves. Their definition of love may be claiming you or saying I love you, but cheats and does not show any attention or affection. If that is the love you want, then hey, who is to judge, but if not, then it is time to reevaluate what it means for you. It is okay to teach someone how to love you only if they are truly invested in growing with you, treating you right, and wanting more. If they are only interested in taking from you then it is time to let them go only if that is what you want. There is no definitive definition or way of love as it differs for each person. The concept is to know and understand what love is to and for you so you can have it. Your definition of love can be a homie and friend, someone that is supportive of your dreams, a mate that provides stability, etc. Again, it is defined by your morals and values in what YOU deserve, want, and need. When you embrace and live in self-love, you have all that you need. You may want someone to share your life with, but you may not necessarily need them. This may take some time to understand, but it is a game changer for those that will walk that path. This does not mean you are against love or relationships, or the cliché, "I don't need a man or woman." It just means you have standards and you are not willing to sacrifice for someone who does not mean you well. Love yourself first and you will see how your perception of love changes and understand why you deserve more. It will make you see your worth and how priceless it is.

Reflect

_____

_____

_____

_____

_____

_____

_____

_____

_____

_____

_____

_____

_____

_____

_____

_____

_____

Love is a feeling that can be indescribable, but there are feelings you can associate it with that makes it feel right. Like someone who treats you like a princess, spoils you like a brat, values you as a queen, and sees you as a goddess. A love that brings nostalgia of childhood. Playing tag in the summer heat, the smell of the first summer's BBQ, the first dip in the pool, warmth of the sun after being in the A/C all day, and your feet in the cool sand on a hot day. A love like the beginning of spring, the refreshing air, rainstorms, warm weather, and the feeling of happiness. A love like the smell of leaves in the fall, a crisp breeze while being comforted by a hoodie. Love like Halloween, hot apple cider, pumpkin picking, hot chocolate, and the scenery in a small town that truly represents the change of seasons. A love like the first snowflake in the winter, the coziness of your bed while snuggling under the cover while rubbing your feet in bed on a cold day. What does love remind you of and how does it make you feel? If you are unsure, do not fret— you will get there— hopefully by the end of this book.

Reflect

_____

_____

_____

_____

_____

_____

_____

_____

_____

_____

_____

_____

_____

_____

_____

_____

The art of turning your pain into power starts with changing your perception with an uncomfortable self-perspective. How can you turn your pain into power if all you know is pain? Your art is the soul's expression that may not be able to be put into words. Confusing to some. Familiarity to others. Relatable to the misunderstood. Crazy to those who have a complex relationship with their soul. How can you turn your pain into power if all you know is pain? That is the million-dollar question with a complicated answer. One of the ways is to stop self-sabotaging. Self-sabotaging can be remaining in places or around people that are unhealthy for you. Your mind-set can be self-sabotaging. Limiting yourself with constricted and/or confined thoughts/beliefs. Going against yourself and treating yourself like the enemy is self-sabotaging.

Why are you your biggest downfall when you should be your biggest strength and supporter. Maintain your power by believing in yourself. For those that did not or does not have supportive or positive people in their lives, this may be tough to embrace, so you need to turn that pain into power and be your strength. Be the person toward yourself that you desire from others. When you do not have any one to talk to or confide in, talk and confide in yourself. There is no judgement, you are your own safe space. Only we can down ourselves with negative self-talk. Sometimes talking to ourselves can bring enlightenment and awareness. You can allow yourself to be free and vent all that is within you. Sometimes, we give ourselves the best advice. You may always be the sound board and safe place for others, you may feel and been told you give the best advice. It sucks when you do not take your own advice. Why is it a struggle to trust ourselves when others can and turn to us easily? One reason can be is we lack belief and confidence due to choices we have made in the past by going against our feelings/thoughts/instincts but think about those times and the factors that contributed to it. Now you can make decisions and talk yourself into a more positive direction as you have the power to do so by honoring your higher self. Your higher self may seem like a critic, but it is not. Your higher self wants to turn your pain into power so you can always operate within your highest good. Your higher self is a voice of reason with constructive criticism that is trying to lead you to the best choices and not down the path of destruction. Trust yourself by believing in yourself and your abilities.

Reflect

_____

_____

_____

_____

_____

_____

_____

_____

_____

_____

_____

_____

_____

_____

_____

_____

_____

_____

You ever ended your workday and planned to go to the gym, grocery shopping, mall, etc., but on the way you run into a traffic jam. You are in the traffic jam longer than anticipated and lose the motivation to do what you set out to do. Sometimes, we can take a detour that takes us out of the way. This applies to your journey. You may lose the motivation because of the traffic in your life that comes in the form of work, friends, family, children, or even school. So, you may need to take a detour that can be to recluse, isolate, or change the environment. Do not look at the detour as an obstacle, but a change of pace to help you see clearly in front of you and consider alternatives. The detour helps you avoid the traffic, but provides you gems along the way. Along the detour, you might see nice houses as you drive through a residential area or you might stroll through neighborhoods you are not fond of and see what you are glad you are not living in. The scenery might motivate you to keep going as you see what you have accomplished or inspire you to grow as you see what you eventually desire to have. The scenery may be different, but it is needed to help keep you motivated. Become motivated by what is ahead, not what you are leaving behind. Leave the traffic as it is only a distraction. Take that detour and look at it from a different perspective. Work with yourself, not against yourself.

Reflect

What holds some people back from success and going toward their goals is fear. Fear of seeing others "fail," fear of seeing others not strive for their full potential, fear of being successful. What do you mean the fear of seeing someone else fail? Isn't that a personal problem? Yes and no. If you look to others for inspiration or motivation, you look at their success and the glamour of what they created, so that gives you hope to strive for your own dreams. Yet, when you see the lack of success in others regardless of what they are attempting to accomplish, you may become fearful that you, too, may fail. Maybe they do not have the skills, determination, or whatever is needed to succeed, but that should not stop you. Look at their "failure" as motivation to get all your ducks in a row and use it as a teaching tool on what not to do when your success is coming slow. You will use those examples of how to maintain and keep going despite the uncertain outcome. We live in a society that tells us we must work a 9 to 5 for thirty plus years and then be able to retire to enjoy life. Not true! That is an outdated mind-set and it does not apply to everyone, especially those with a gift that needs to be put into the world. How do I know I have this gift you may ask. If it has been sitting inside of you, on your mind, and you feel lost/stagnant because you are not working toward it, then you have a gift the world needs. Your gift may not be for everyone, but do not take offense. It is for those that need it. It is for those that need the inspiration to turn their pain into power, those that need direction or a role model to believe in themselves. It is for YOU. It is to help create the life you want and desire. It is to help you move past what is not and has not worked for you. It is for you to believe in and trust yourself with. Not everyone is meant to see the vision you have, but if you see it that is all that matters. Be that voice of reason, hope, and fulfillment that brings life to yourself and maybe others. Embrace the challenges as you would embrace the achievements. Challenges help you grow and achievements make you appreciate what you have obtained and the path you have chosen to take. Let fear be a motivating factor not a blockage.

Reflect

_____

_____

_____

_____

_____

_____

_____

_____

_____

_____

_____

_____

_____

_____

_____

_____

_____

You ever feel lost or stuck in life? You ever prayed for clarity or a way out? When we pray, we desire immediate results, but that is not how life goes. You may start crying, praying with all your heart, and begging for change. For some, the answers are there because they were heard, but many of us learn the hard way. Some only see the signs if it is clear as day and we are told "THIS IS YOUR SIGN!!" When you do not take heed to the "signs" you have been praying for, life can become difficult. Your higher source/self may create uncomfortable circumstances in your life to help you see what needs to be done due to you not acting. It could be in terms of losing your job, home, ending of a relationship, etc., so you can be forced unto the right path. The more you ignore it, the more difficult and uncomfortable it will be. That initial sign may be subtle and not as direct as you may want it. It may be in an unexpected form, so you dismiss it. The dismissal only activates the trials and tribulations because you apparently can only hear in CAPS LOCK forms. You can only receive in strife because you are hardheaded and lack the faith needed to move forth. Yes, this generates strength and resilience, but it does not have to be this hard all the time. God/your higher self does not want to be hard on you all the time, as they know the harshness you have endured, so they may show you in ways that are gentle. They are trying to teach you gentleness within yourself, but you only understand through hardships, so that is what they bring into your life to help you see. STOP BEING HARDHEADED. I know it is hard, but you should be gentle with yourself. You do not need a hard exterior all the damn time. You need softness, which can allow peace and comfort into your life. I am sure you want an easier life, so learn to take heed when it is offered. I know it is difficult to discern whether it is a sign or not, but that is when you walk in faith and take the chance. If it is not a sign, then use that discernment to walk away or go a different route.

Trust your intuition, that is why you were gifted with it. Whether big or small, take that motivation or blessing and go big. You ever experienced being depleted after working a job you do not really want, so after work you go home and be "lazy" or do the bare minimum. This can be your sign to make those changes. Lose that weight, stop drinking, stop smoking, kick that nigga/bitch out your house, tell them kids to shut up. Whatever it is, that can be your sign to just do it and stand on it. Fulfillment does not come with just laying around wallowing in self-pity, it comes with doing the work and challenging yourself. You will continue to feel unfulfilled when you are not doing what is in your heart or taking heed to those signs. Turn it into power and live the authentic version of yourself.

Reflect

Is your authentic self only present when the world is quiet or at night? It requires a lot of time, discipline, and energy to create quietness when the world is chaotic. When you have a regular job, but also trying to achieve your dreams, creating the quietness during chaos is necessary. For many, that means going within to create stillness during the daytime and not letting the world distract you from what needs to be accomplished. This allows you to have some sort of authenticity. Being authentic means ridding yourself of the confinements and restrictions life gives you. Being authentic means living within your best self and operating out a place that brings you peace. When there is no peace, you become chaotic. That can mean altering your environment to create what allows you to be your truest self. It may take patience and discipline for some to learn. It can take isolation, reclusion, and going within the environment that allows authenticity. Not being your authentic self means you are restricting yourself and it can prevent you from that dream job/career, relationship, college major, or whatever you want out of life. Being your authentic self allows you to be who and what you are with no regrets. Do not allow life, work, etc., to stop you from being YOU. By doing so, you are giving your power to someone/something else to control. Take control and be you. Only you know your authentic self and that takes patience for some to learn. It takes the isolation, being reclusive, being within the environment that allows you to be authentic. Once you have become disciplined within creating an environment for your authentic self, you can showcase it in the world. Not being authentic prevents you from accomplishing your dreams. Being the real you can be scary when you hide it all the time, but it is frustrating when you live a lie and wear a mask. So what option are you going to take? The REAL you or the façade?

Reflect

Self-love is stripping yourself naked by removing all your layers and connecting with yourself. It is being vulnerable with the essence of you. Self-love is gaining valuable knowledge, wisdom, and strength of yourself and life. Self-love is solely centered on you and the elements that makes you valuable. There is no correct way to look, speak, or act when you embody self-love, but the way you feel about yourself is important. Self-love is reprogramming your beliefs, morals, thoughts, etc., about yourself and reconstructing your self-perception to nurture within. It is eliminating unhealthy habits, releasing what does not serve you, being gentle, and loving yourself. It is learning to give yourself credit and props often and seeing yourself from a different lens. There is the superficial aspect of self-love of telling yourself "I love you" in the mirror all the time and pampering yourself with materialistic things. Yes, this is helpful for many, but look beyond that and dig deeper. Express the abyss of yourself and love yourself along the journey. Self-love is knowing your worth and power without needing or seeking the validation from others. It is about YOU. When operating out of self-love, there will be times when you have to make uncomfortable decisions for your best interest. The battle will be between your heart, head, and past self. Each have valid points and reasons, but your higher self will make the best decision to protect each facet of you. This is the goal and objective of self-love, to put yourself first and love you throughout the good and bad times. My self-love journey derived in different stages. Sometimes I feel like a teenager experimenting with life on a journey to newness while being unadulterated with freedom to explore myself. I am trying new things and being open to adventures within my safe zone. I feel the adult version of self-love will be when I am the version that I envision myself. More comfortable with myself and free of the burdens I am releasing.

It is about having a better quality of life by tapping into your higher self and embracing it. Being cool with a version of yourself you have yet to meet. This person sees the best in you and wants you to step out of your shell and into the world. This person is someone you admire and will fall deeply in love with as you grow and develop a relationship. Trust your higher self and claim that energy. You will be meeting yourself for the first time, so nurture the bond with gentleness and ease and allow the flower to bloom without fear. Your higher self is not afraid, but you are. Your higher self is waiting for you to emerge, so what are you waiting for?

Reflect

_____

_____

_____

_____

_____

_____

_____

_____

_____

_____

_____

_____

_____

_____

_____

_____

_____

Do not fret when your prayers or manifestation has not produced immediate results. I know most of us want instant gratification, but life does not work like that. What if what you are seeking requires more healing. Yes, it can be frustrating when you have been working on yourself day in and day out. I know you are tired and want to see the fruits of your healing but be patient. From a basic perception, healing is only understanding and processing what we have been through, but healing includes one's heart. I know you may think it is the same, but it is not. You cannot do one without the other. I mean you can, but are you truly healed? Get to the root of your hearts pain, desires, etc., to truly heal and mend those inner wounds. Healing from relationships and rejection is one thing, but you have to release that hurt from your heart or it will always fester and never heal. Once you let that pain go then you can truly pray and manifest with an open heart and wait patiently for those blessings. Look at it like this, you cannot appreciate blessings or manifest from a broken heart or spirit. What you will produce will not be fulfilling, especially not when embodied with pain and hurt, so healing will help release those blockages and bring your dreams to reality. Praying for marriage and/or children with an unhealed spirit will not automatically make life better for you if you manifest it while still in pain. I am sure your marriage and children will feel the effects of it and so will you, so take the time to heal then pray for those blessings. You do not want to bring anyone into your hurt as it can potentially hurt them. This does not only pertain to people, but it also includes whatever you wish for, so keep that in mind.

Reflect

That thing you desire so bad, that you pray for daily and beg for, may be delayed. Delayed for a reason. Do not go, let me explain. Think of that dream, goal, desire you have, now think of someone you know that may have that same thing. You may feel they are experiencing the blessing or opportunity that seems to keep passing you by regardless of what it is. Now, let us look from a different standpoint. Have you ever considered you are able to see, witness, or observe that blessing from someone else because you are being given the blueprint for your foundation? Maybe you have not been blessed yet because you still have work to do. The insight of this may be a hard pill to swallow, but you are being blessed with the opportunity to prepare for success. No matter if it is a relationship, job, relocating, whatever it is, you are being prepared. You are being given the opportunity to prepare for the blessing. You may witness the rise and/or fall of those that have what you are working toward. This preparation is the blueprint and foundation of your success. That relationship you want will come when you learn what you truly need from a partner because right now you may be struggling with boundaries, self-worth/love, or other unhealed things. The relationship you desire requires you to be a better version of yourself. The job you really want may not require a degree and you have the experience, but going back to school will advance you in that career. You might need to change your habits at work like stop gossiping, complaining, etc. This is just a broad spectrum of examples, but I am sure you get the gist. This is just a premiere with more to come because what you may be blessed with can be far beyond what you can perceive in the moment. The sky is not the limit, it is only if you let it be. Take the time to learn from the delay to see what you need to do. Be patient as the best results come from hard work and take their time. Trying to force things in life with a heavy energy will be detrimental. Having a light and flowing energy allows things to come with ease. Seeds cannot grow on unfertile ground or cement, just like your blessings cannot unfold with a desperate energy. Change the energy to welcome the fertilization process and watch the seed grow in naturally. Sometimes there is a delay with the growth but know everything will work out in due time.

Reflect

_____
_____
_____
_____
_____
_____
_____
_____
_____
_____
_____
_____
_____
_____
_____
_____
_____

Invest in yourself so you can invest in your future. Investing in yourself mentally, emotionally, and spiritually is a vital component. If you fail to invest in you, then who will? Invest in your passion. Invest in your beliefs. Invest in your gift(s). Stop treating your dreams like a Sunday night when you know the weekend is over and dreading going to work tomorrow. Stop treating your dream like a Monday morning, being at a job you do not like, and you are ready for the weekend. Babes, it is only 8:30 a.m. on Monday morning, you just got to work. Instead, treat your dreams like a Friday when you are excited for the weekend to rest or do whatever you planned to do. Treat your dreams like an upcoming holiday with a long weekend ahead. Treat it like the day before your week-long vacation or the last day of your two-week notice. Be excited!!!! Yes, it may be scary, but be excited and look forward to it. Instead of feeling overwhelmed by your dream and the process, let's change the perspective. You know how you prepare for a vacation? Deciding where you want to go, who is going, how long, determining the means of transportation, keeping up with the weather forecast, booking flights/hotels, etc. You also need to do some shopping (clothes, luggage, shoes, etc.), get your hair done, nails done— whatever else. This is the preparation period of your trip. You also put in a time off request. So, the preparation to your dream is getting all the information you need, researching, getting documents together, the whole nine yards. The time off request would be equivalent to getting prepared in advance for what is to come. The next phase is the traveling. You are traveling to your destination whether by car, train, boat, bus, foot. Now it is time for you to travel to the next phase of your dream, which is laying the groundwork and getting the foundation established with deadlines to get everything together. Once you arrive at your destination, the fun begins. The fun is living your dream because you started the process by believing in your dream and yourself. The idea is no longer dangling in your head, in a notebook, or in conversations you had with others. You are now prepared mentally, physically, emotionally, and possibly financially for the next step. The preparation and travel is complete, now it is time for the live action in which you should be enjoying, just like your vacation. Now the vacation is over and you return home. The return trip is revising and adjusting where needed. You are back to a clean home, excited to sleep in your bed again, and relish in your accomplishments as your dream continues to live out. You finally invested in yourself and Mondays are no longer a drag and Fridays are not the only days to be excited about. Congratulations!!!!!

Reflect

_____

_____

_____

_____

_____

_____

_____

_____

_____

_____

_____

_____

_____

_____

_____

_____

_____

The time to elevate is now. Why? Because you know it is time to. Time to elevate from the past, hurt, confusion, and all that weighs you down. Elevating in this context means to take charge of your life. Stop the procrastination and playing games with yourself. You may be used to people playing games with you, but it ends now. Take the good with the bad and the ups with the downs. Elevating means you do not let the tough times destroy you but make you stronger than ever. Stop putting out that fire that burns within and let the flame light the way. That flame is your spark and you ignite it with elevating into the amazing person you are. Be the light to your future and do not let the flame burn out.

Reflect

When you are a vessel to deliver a message remember the message will not be for everyone, but those that are meant to receive it. You were chosen to be the messenger because no one else can deliver it like you. You have that special gift and skill needed for the job, and you are the blessing for those that hear it. So, do not falter when the message may not be received; you did your job, and the task is complete. Many of us are an inspiration and voice of reason to others struggling and in need of a safe place to vent. The downside is some of you do not have someone or a safe place to go. Maybe your safe place is through yourself when helping others. You ever talk to someone who is venting to you and you give some really good advice/feedback, then BAM, you inspired yourself. You gave yourself the answer/solution you were looking for without even thinking about it. In that moment, your focus was on someone else, but you were able to help yourself along the way. Maybe you need to sit with yourself and be vulnerable. Some may think it is crazy to engage in self-talk, but it should be the safest place for you. Once you truly realize you can trust yourself, you can start to depend on you more. You stop second guessing yourself and become more confident with relying on yourself for answers. This does not mean you will not or cannot have someone else to confide in, but you will not be desperate for answers. You may vent for additional advice, but you will not give your power away to someone else to solve or have the need to depend on others for validation or help, but more so for guidance or confirmation

Reflect

We falter sometimes when working on ourselves or going for that goal/dream. Some people's strength comes from trauma, heartache, anger, etc., and when the things that catapults you to move is not there, you may feel lost, stagnant, or uninspired. In those moments, life can be like a lake/river. The lake/river can be calm and beautiful or it can be rough with tides and heavy currents. When all you know is strife, you seem to excel in the ripples and currents as you learned to ride those rough waters with experience. Yet, when the lake/river is clear, calm, and serene, you become disheveled. This is a time to focus as things become clearer for you. You have the time to think without the need for an emergency plan or life jackets because you have nothing to fear except peace. Learn to admire the beauty of rest and peace. Although you are used to the dangerous waters that is rough and terrifying, adjust to enjoying yourself and life. Embrace relaxation, restoration, your accomplishments, and growth. This can inspire you to want more days like this and strive for it. This can help eliminate burnout, stress, survival mode, flight or fight, and mental/physical turmoil. Allow these times to connect with self and see life from a different perspective.

Reflect

Life gives us detours to show us a different path. It may seem like a nuisance at first, but it can be a blessing in disguise. Think of it like this. You are shopping, it is crowded, and the lines are long. You just want to get home, relax, and do whatever it is that you want, but these current circumstances are delaying that. You can leave and not accomplish anything or be patient and not rush. So, what the hell, you decide to wait. What if waiting is life's way of slowing you down. Maybe it is a sign you need to slow down and take it easy. As you wait, you people watch, see something on clearance that catches your eye, or check your emails. You can also self-reflect on so many things that you just did not have time to process or deliberate on before, especially since you have no control of the situation. You may get a second wind and stop at additional stores or try a new restaurant. Waiting brings forth patience. You feel calm, unrushed, and relaxed. You are not even rushing home to do your normal activities because you are trying something new. Take delight in this and implement waiting/patience when your body, mind, soul, and/or life tells you.

Reflect

Strength can be another component of self-love; growing spiritually, sensually, mentally, emotionally, being
balanced, selfish, with love, laughter, and good memo-
ries. It means being the person you have always dreamt
of, doing things you have always dreamt of, understanding you can create/manifest the life you want.
Understanding what you really want/need. Living and
enjoying life doing what you want and not beating
yourself up if it does not fit the "norm." It means exploring and experiencing life in its truest form that is
not based on trials and tribulations, tests, or lessons
from the universe/God, but living as it was meant to be
lived. Yes, there will be hiccups and shit as life continues to happen, but your strength will get you through it
better than being strong. Some battles are meant to be
fought with strength, not being strong (fight or flight/

survival mode). Strength uses confidence, wisdom, intuition, guidance, and self-awareness. Being strong uses negative energy, fear, anger, confusion, and low vibration. Being strong does not allow you to be patient or understanding, but hard and aggressive. Operate with strength and the gentle delicacies with your battles to provide you with clarity and softness.

Reflect

Comfort zone can keep you stagnant and limited in what you can and will do. Your safe zone allows you to explore, be happy, comfortable in your surroundings, and enjoy positive experiences the comfort zone restricts. Safe zone keeps you safe with your limits, which is okay. Going out of your comfort zone at times can result in depression, anxiety, fear, toxic thoughts, and doing things you are not safe or comfortable with. Your safe zone allows you to come out of your shell at your own pace and use discernment that promotes growth and freedom. The safe zone is all about you. It is not about feeling rushed or forced to do things, but taking your time to understand what is that you want, enjoyment, and how to achieve it by being your best self. Feeling forced or obligated to come out of your comfort zone may have you react out of fear and character. That can make you feel uncomfortable, unsafe, and enter the world with a façade as it is not something you want to do. So, take your time and learn what your safe zone is and how you want to explore life.

Reflect

Do not forget to appreciate all the lessons and experiences you have had in life regardless good or bad. It was essential for you to go through for growth, self-love, and maturity. Although those bad times may feel like an essential crisis to your life, it is not always the case. It is vital for the transformation. Transformation is needed to elevate. The transformation starts by building a relationship with yourself as this is a lifelong relationship you have to continually work on. You cannot ghost it, walk away from it, take a break, or stop because it is embedded in you. The transformation starts by evolving like a caterpillar into a butterfly. Evolving into a butterfly can be a challenge. Sometimes it is hard to morph into the butterfly when you are comfortable in the cocoon or being a caterpillar. Becoming the butterfly is a new sense of freedom, journey, delight, joy, and release that may be uncomfortable to embrace/ accept. Being the butterfly takes time as one develops an understanding of their safe zone. The caterpillar phase is your comfort zone. You mainly isolate, recluse, and is known to be a hermit. You do not like change as it may be scary for you, but you desire a new sense of freedom. This is where you morph into the cocoon. You are in a contemplative mode and down time is needed to process. You start to connect with yourself to help you grasp what it is you want. This is time for evalua- tion, reflection, and the desire for change. The cocoon is in the middle of change and stagnation. This varies from person to person, but let's say you are an introvert and want to be more social. You start to entertain the idea of getting out more, searching for events, and ideas on what to do. As a caterpillar, you feel safe because you do not have to deal with people, experience social anxiety, or anxiety in general being around others or in crowds. Your definition of becoming a butterfly can start by taking small steps such as going to happy hour after work, or a quiet bar/club where you can relax and learn to get comfortable around people. In most cases, conversations can spark while at a bar/club, so it allows you to practice if you are up to it. You can try other things if bars/clubs is not your thing. Maybe going to an event like a museum, comedy show, paint-n-sip, or whatever you may like. You can try it out a few times to scope the scene and get comfortable. As time goes on, you may strike up a general conversation with others, even if it is small talk. This is to get you out of your comfort zone, but to stay within a safe one for you. The goal is not to rush or overwhelm yourself, but to take it slow and easy while exploring the world safely. As you morph into a butterfly, you try new things, life is exciting, and you are no longer scared to fly.

Reflect

After healing, you might go through a crisis that is equivalent to a mid-life crisis. This crisis is triggered by realizing the time, life, energy, etc., that was lost/wasted and cannot be returned to you. This is what you may feel or think as you look ahead and may feel more time was spent on trauma than what you feel you may have left to enjoy. Life slows down when you are healed as you now have time. Time to take things slow, time to enjoy life, time to just be. Before, life went by fast as you were conflicted and going through endless internal battles. You were not focused on life; you were focused on the trauma. Unfortunately, the "best" years of your life was not the best, and you are now older and may feel your youth is gone. That is a myth. You may experience more youth now than in the past because the trauma was aging you mentally, emotionally, and possibly physically. Now that you have released that, your youth is restored. Do not think about your age and what society has conditioned us to think or believe we should be at a certain age, but think about how you feel and what you want to feel. If you want to live like a teenager, so be it. No, it does not mean being imma- ture, but being carefree and experiencing the world free of shackles. The shackles for teenagers are their parents but for you it is the past. So live life as if you are free of parental supervision and wanting to find yourself in this big old world with endless opportunities with so much life ahead of you.

Reflect

You may experience conflict when it is between your heart and head. Your heart is acting out of love, but your head is acting out of logic. When it comes to people that hurt you there is conflict between your heart and head. Remember your heart is full of love, but it does not mean that other person is operating out of love. Sometimes you have to reason with logic as it helps eliminate issues your heart cannot let go of because of love. This conflict can also make you second guess yourself, which may upset you. Although it may be difficult at times during these encounters, make those tough decisions with self-love and faith in your highest self to decide the correct path. With self-love, you are operating out of love for yourself and logically putting yourself first and making the best decision for you and you only. Learn to balance your heart and head because failing to do so will always be a tug of war. Allow empathy when needed but know when to take a step back to assess the situation for what it is.

Reflect

_____

_____

_____

_____

_____

_____

_____

_____

_____

_____

_____

_____

_____

_____

_____

_____

_____

_____

As you grow, your environment may look different although nothing has changed. The difference is how you look at your environment as an evolved person. The same environment may reflect the past with no growth or a present and future with endless opportunities, it depends on the new path/journey you are taking. Sometimes the environment becomes a dilapidated, scroungy place in your eyes and a desire and seek out the change needed as a new person. It is okay to be still as you break out of your cocoon to adjust to the new you. You are allowing yourself to take it all in before you share your new self to the world. Getting to know the new you is crucial before discovering a new way of life and living. The new you is discovering life for the first time and you should embrace it as an adventure to explore as you please. Just imagine the freedom you can have rediscovering life from a healed, loved, courageous, joyful, and unlimited authentic soul. Allow yourself the time to adjust, embrace, and become comfortable with the new version of yourself. Having expectations can result in you going back within as you may experience fear of the unknown or the reality is not what you anticipated. This is not a race, so do not place any constraints on yourself that can create a barrier for growth to occur naturally.

Reflect

Who heals you when you are always healing others and you do not have time to focus on yourself? You might even have to heal from those you heal and/or toxic people in general. Such as realizing then need to heal yourself, after constantly healing yourself from dealing with the same people who are not good for you. Some people are fueled into healing via pain, hurt, anger, and confusion others bring into their life. Use those emotions to connect stronger to yourself spirituality. This is the step to understanding and appreciating self-love and knowing you need to heal and making it a priority. You might get someone to heal you, but not in a way you expect or how you heal others. At times, pain or motivation from others can sprout your healing.

Nonetheless, your healing journey is different from others and will be only crafted in the manner perfectly for you.

Reflect

Sometimes your blessings are paused when you have takers and leeches in your life. At times, you will have to wait until that type of energy is removed from your life to be blessed. When you have a good/sharing spirit, you will give away what was meant only for you to those that do not deserve it. Now you robbed yourself, but blessed someone who probably would not have done the same in return. Your inability to say no can stop your blessings. When you have given to others without anything in return, it is normal to be upset because no one has done for you what you have done for them. Just know, you will be blessed in return when you need them, not when you want them. Life is about reciprocity; what you give is what you receive, good and bad. Those blessings are being reserved for the tough times and will be given in unexpected ways. Those blessings will be returned in the same manner you blessed others with kindness. Remember what is for you is for you and not for everyone. Be selfish with your blessings, especially if you worked for it. But if you feel compelled to share, only share with those with a kind and genuine spirit. Here is another notion to consider about those you surround yourself with. I am sure we all heard the cliche that not everyone is meant to go with you on your journey. Once you have developed a relationship whether intimate/ friendship, etc., and that person or people have helped you grow and whatever ways, it may be difficult to let them go. Feeling that person/ people were pivotal to your advancement but were only there for that season for a purpose. That purpose may not be realized in the beginning. As you become more centered and in tune with yourself you will realize their purpose. It will be difficult to let them go due to the relationship developed, especially if they were a catalyst to your enhancement. Sometimes they are not meant to go on the journey any longer. This concept may be hard to grapple in that moment. Once you become grounded within yourself and in that calm water you will understand. You may want them around, but they have done their job. Do not be afraid to enmesh yourself with like-minded people. It is difficult to maintain relationships when you do not have much in common. If you are an artist, wouldn't you want to be around other artists for inspiration and an outlet to share your craft? If being at peace is your mantra, then you should want to surround yourself with others who are at peace. Do not destroy what you gave/put so much into having by opening the door for destructive people to invade your peace or space.

Reflect

A man exploring and savoring the uncharted delicacies of your mind, body, and soul is a renowned type of intimacy. His tongue is the guide whether it is to taste or talk. His hands are explorers of your goddess temple as he cherishes your divine territories. His knowledge and wisdom keep the fountain overflowing with love and nourishment for him to drink from. Only a real man has the armor to unlock this mystic continent of its true power, blessing, and beauty.

Reflect

He reminded me of love. He reminded me of the feelings that came with love. He reminded me that a man and make me blush and feel desired. He taught me self-love and unconditional love for myself. He showed me how I have neglected myself for all these years by pouring into others. Unrequited love, love that was taken advantage of, love that had no real intentions except to break me. Not only did he remind me how to love a man intimately, but he also taught me that I should be loved just the same. He taught me through his actions. Actions of disappearing, lies, lack of trust, confusion, and childish behavior. What I learned was, from now on if a man does not love me as much as I love myself, he does not deserve me or my love. He taught me how to let him go while still loving him, but loving me more than he ever can, will, or try to. Does he know our love could have moved mountains. That our love could have erased the pain from the past. Our love was the epitome of real love. That love broke barriers to my soul and laid the foundation for a lifetime of love. The love was peace, serene, safe, and secure within our hearts. Does he know how painful it was to let that love go? To release him back to the universe and sever those ties? Does he know? No, he does not because I took that pain and turned it into power. The power of self-love.

Reflect

Having a clean slate of love means energetically returning the love you have for someone back to them, mainly
if it was toxic. It means energetically rejecting the love/
feelings they had/have for you and returning to sender.
You have an abundance of self-love, which overflows
and can be given to others. You do not need to bring
in the past love of others. Meaning the love that was in
one relationship may not be the love required or needed
for the next. You do not love everyone the same, so do
not expect to have the same love for the next person. If
you were in an abusive relationship, that was not true
love, and not the same love you bring into a healthy
relationship. The love you gave when you were broken
is not the same love you give when healed. So, release
those limiting beliefs on love and learn to teach others
how to love you. Your mate who is affectionate might

show love differently than your ex who did not know about real love. Be gentle with yourself and others as you learn to love in many ways, but remember not everyone deserves your love.

Reflect

Have you ever given your power away and realized afterward you lost it. To get it back, you must know the power you hold and how much it is worth. I gave my power to people without realizing how much they benefited from it. My power gave them strength they did not have because when I left so did their strength. I put them on a pedestal as I watched them in their strength not understanding it was my power that fueled them. Hell, I gave them more credit than God, spirit, and the universe did in that relationship. All along, I should have been putting myself on a pedestal and praising myself (and of course God/spirit). Now that I know the power I hold, I will treasure it as a priceless antique. I will treasure and value myself as a goddess of strength, power, loyalty, and love. What is your power and who are you a goddess of? You are a goddess of yourself and of love, so do not give your power away to low vibrational people.

Reflect

There are people who want to change their whole life around, and feel relocating is the best option. There is a cliche that says, "you go wherever you go." What some people may interpret is you still have certain ways about you, so unless you change that, things will still be the same regardless of the relocation. Yes, that may be true for some, but for others, they need the change of environment. They may need to separate themselves from negative, abusive, toxic people, or environment. They may need a fresh start to surround themselves with positive people. Where they were could've stunted their growth with limited opportunities. They may need that fresh start to be who they truly are as their current location may be hindering them from growing. They may lack the support or ability to flourish as they could be surrounded by people stuck in their ways and against change. So do not hold back and keep yourself stuck, learn, grow, develop, and take the risk. It may be a struggle at first, even overwhelming and confusing, but do what is best for you. Do not allow others to dictate your life, as they may be projecting from their limited outlook. I am not saying to make unwise decisions, but do what is best for you. I could not live life like those I've seen as they were not prospering and do the same shit all the time because they were stuck. I needed more. I begged and pleaded with God and the universe for many years to get me out of that rut. When they did, it was not a pleasurable experience, but one that allowed me not to turn back as I have been blessed. It is not all roses, believe that. It is hard, but for me it was worth it. What others may want for me is not in my best interest or path, so choose the path that is right for you. You may find the support, love, and guidance you need in that change. Do not forget you still have to work on yourself, or nothing will change for the better. Sometimes change is needed to fully heal, so changing your surrounding is necessary and possible.

Reflect

Is sex and intimacy equivalent to pain, hurt, being un-comfortable, and not letting others know we combined our bodies together? For some this scan be the case due to toxic and traumatic experiences. This ties to my youth/childhood by being in uncomfortable situations that stripped me of my innocence. As an adult, I longed for intimacy and sex that felt right, that felt good, and not being hidden from others. The feeling of safe. I was never safe, but I had to protect myself by giving into these advances from people who took away my essence. I had to mentally accept it and be comfortable with it. In teenage/adult years, all I knew was giving myself away in all forms because that is what I learned in my youth. I only knew to give away something that was supposed to be treasured, but I learned the value of me because I never got to know it. I never got to experience the value of my innocence because I did not have it for very long. I guess I am still searching for my value and innocence in some instances. I want back what was taken from me when I was defenseless and could not fight. I accepted that I'll never get that time back, so now I have to understand what I'm truly searching for. I am no longer searching for the orgasm that will make me feel like a woman. I am no longer searching for the man to make me feel valued and wanted other than for sex. I am searching for the woman who did not have a chance to grow up, but was forced to. I am searching for the woman that is no longer scared or allows herself to be put into circumstances because she knows no other way. I am searching for this woman because it is time to be free, be happy, and healed. Let go of the hurt, pain, distrust, and anger. I had to let go of this mask of the cloaking the woman and wounded lost child. The child that hides because every time they emerge, they are hurt all over again. This is the child afraid to explore because of the bad people who do not care about their innocence, life, feelings, safety, or being. This is the child that experienced adult situations and is angered from it. As an adult, I was still angry. I felt like I have been an adult most of my life. I am tired. I want to play. I want to make friends. I want boyfriends. I want to date. I want to explore and experience womanhood. In my 30's, I feel older than I actually am. I have always had to be ahead of my time to protect myself (at least try to), so I missed out so much in life. All because some fucker wanted to use my innocence to satisfy their needs and I was left emotionally, mentally, financially, physically, and psychologically to deal with it. I was furious, but I took my power back and started living life for me.

Reflect

Understanding boundaries prevents you from being manipulated and taken advantage of. It allows you to see things from a different perspective, but maintain yourself and respect by keeping those boundaries in place. Do not allow your past experiences and that mind-set aide in your understanding of others and their ways be your downfall. Your boundaries show others that you are non-judgmental, but will not allow nonsense to trespass on your peace. You now set the standard of what you will and will not accept into your life. Your boundaries have a password and only then can people get through. This does not mean you have to have a tough exterior, but you are more mindful of what you will not tolerate.

Reflect

There is no syllabus on your life, so you may need to establish one. The syllabus for you comes with instructions, a timeframe, etc. Life does not. You create your syllabus. You are your own instructor. There are no grades, but there are learning experiences and lessons. Only you can determine the outcome. You have a transcript of your life, so you can review it to see where more attention is required, areas of struggle/greatness, and what you want to include. What would you want on your life's resume. Like applying for a job, you make a resume to show why you deserve it, skill set, qualifications, and what you seek from that new position. You will make one for you. This will also require a cover letter to yourself and God/higher power if you choose. You will review the qualifications, etc., to see how you are the best fit. After reviewing, you will determine where you need additional training in your life. Training is to help with your character development and self-improvement. Just like a job, you will need to be trained in areas that are unfamiliar or needs some fine tuning. Give yourself credit where you excel and be willing to grow in areas you lack the skillset to advance.

Reflect

Some roadblocks are meant to prepare you for your future instead of impeding your growth. Do not look at this as something to deter you, but to strengthen and motivate you. So, when they say the devil hears you and to keep your mouth shut, sometimes you need to speak it aloud so God and spirit hears you. Sometimes it is not the devil, but God or your spirit guides giving you direction. This is confirmation you are serious and God knows that you are ready. Be ready for the preparation period because there are things that you need to learn and obtain to move forth. Do not let it discourage you, let it motivate and inspire you. God will not allow the devil to conquer you, but allow you the ability to conquer the devil. Although the devil is listening, God is listening, too, so walk with faith and allow yourself to accomplish what it is that you want. Allow this to be a reminder and inspiration to continue to do what it is that you want and what you need to. Look at it to motivate, not deter you. Knowing that you can conquer the devil regardless of how stealth they are, you can conquer this with strength and faith in a higher power as well as yourself.

Reflect

_____
_____
_____
_____
_____
_____
_____
_____
_____
_____
_____
_____
_____
_____
_____
_____
_____
_____

At times when we have a new concept or venture, we become excited and experience an adrenaline rush. That adrenaline rush gives us the confidence and motivation to work toward whatever we are inspired to do. But once that adrenaline rush goes away, we might back away from that goal and aspiration. That dream or goal becomes delayed or something pushed in the back of the mind for whenever we have the time to come back to it or get that rush again. That adrenaline is to give us that power/ motivation to want to accomplish what we desire, and when that goes away, we need to find a new inspiration. That inspiration was that rush and adrenaline. Although the excitement may be gone, the concept is still there. So, you may have to act on it when inspired so it does not become something you will think back on wondering what could have been. What could have been is grueling to think about when you do not see a dream through. Contemplating what could have prospered is a bitch to sit on when you had the opportunity. Again, life is a gamble as we venture toward those aspirations, thoughts, dreams, or goals. You win some, you lose some, but knowing you put forth the effort, time, and energy to try to see it through is what matters. Our dreams may never make it through and can discourage us from wanting to try again. Do not give up, try as many times to succeed with our life's fulfillment. This is where you allow yourself to be uninhibited and grow beyond your wildest dreams.

Reflect

Again, life is not an easy path. It is filled with trials, tribulations, happiness, sadness, anger, and all sorts of emotions that may be challenging for you to comprehend. The idea is to utilize what you have learned to get ahead. This is not going to be for everyone. It is for people who may feel stuck in life and not sure on how to get ahead, what to do, where to go, or who to turn to. This is where your faith comes into play. When you feel that stagnant then it is time for a change. Sit down within yourself and really analyze what is going on to truly determine why you feel stuck. Change is uncomfortable as it can be unpredictable and something new can be brewing on the horizon. There could be murky waters or a riptide ahead, just be prepared. Allow yourself to hear that message to get that prophecy, allow that change into your life so you can become a better version. Some of us have continued in a career/employ-ment that utilizes some of the skills and gifts that we have but not to the degree in which we need to put it out in the world. Tapping into the best versions of our-selves releases the stagnancy need to help things flow and allows you to take risks. Challenge yourself with optimism because you can handle it. The challenge is growing and encountering parts of you that were never explored. Be inhibited to fulfill your dreams, which may be bigger than anticipated.

Reflect

Sometimes you need support in ways that you never understood from people you never thought you would. Your biggest supporters who should be your family, friends, etc., you would think that it will come for them but sometimes it does not. Sometimes your biggest support come from others that you never expected it to be. Sometimes you just want that support from those that you know that you should and could and be able to depend on. Not all the time in life you need constructive criticism. Yes, you need that constructive criticism but at times you truly need support— you need that encouragement to go forth. Because without encouragement or support where would you be. At times we can be the encouragement, the motivation, and whatever for ourselves so we need that from others. So, when you do not get that support from the others that you need allow yourself to get the support, the encouragement, the motivation from those who are giving it to you. Do not deny yourself this because again that may not come in the form or the people/person that you expected from but it is going to come unexpected. If you have a higher power that you believe in again, they are not going to come to you and tell you things in a form of the way that you expected to but from a place where you do not expect it to. God in your higher source and yourself is not going to always give it to you how you want it. It is going to come in a form unexpected and you must be open and willing to accept it and embrace it. It is hard to accept and it is a challenge for many, but use it to your advantage so you can do what needs to be done for you. Nobody is going to do for you what needs to be done except for you. So, when you get that blessing from God/spirit take full advantage of it because you never know when it is going to come back around. The next person might be your biggest hater, but consider you might also be your biggest critic. You might be the devil in disguise to yourself by not utilizing that support and going with the flow. You will know when that support is for you or not and want to take it or not trust your judgment but trust your intuition. Life is all about experiencing the journey. This journey is what you make of it. Remember life can be a bitch, but you have to use discernment and sound judgment to navigate through any barriers.

Reflect

Sometimes we are the messenger for God. At times we are put in others' lives to give them a message only they are meant to receive. It may seem like we are being used, but we are— by God. That person needed us and we were used, just like some people are used to deliver us a message that we are not ready to hear from God. When we receive the message, we are still not prepared to receive, but it is there. We have to be open to receiving in any form necessary. If not, the message will be delivered in an uncomfortable way, so keep your eyes and ears open when you ask for that message. When you are a vessel to deliver, your message will not be for everyone. Your messages are for those who are meant to receive it. Your message is to give to those who God/ spirit knew needed the message and was unable to hear it from them. So do not falter and worry about who is not receiving the message because it is not for everyone, just know that it is getting to who needs it.

Reflect

Stop looking at things from a tunnel vision perspective. Doubting your abilities can be that thought or voice that makes you reconsider and second guess yourself. You can be your own devil by sabotaging your blessings. Sometimes the blessings are your dreams for example: a book, business idea, change of mind-set. You ever feel like you are experiencing the Groundhog Day affect in your life. That can potentially be you creating that by sounding like a broken record by not doing what it is that you are trying to set yourself up to do and to be. It is self-sabotaging. So, until you are ready to change and act, you will continue to repeat the same cycles. The change comes when you just do it, so go for it, or keep repeating the same cycle. Sometimes for that spark to return in your life, you need to do what is necessary to bring it back. For instance, if you feel like your dreams are deferred, because that spark is gone, it means you are procrastinating. The spark will not return until you are living in your truth. That spark may return to keep you going, it will encourage you to continue to do more. So do not look at it is lack of motivation or inspiration, but time for you to act.

Reflect

Just like a vacation you know you do a lot of preparing to get ready for booking tickets, getting a hotel, a car, making sure you have the money, getting close, your nails done, etc. And then when you go on vacation you get to relax and enjoy your time because you spent so much time preparing for it. So, you know like many before they go on vacation, they make sure that their house is in order so when they return, they do not have much that they need to do besides unpack but everything else is clean and you know you just get to relax. So, think of it like this is after your rest. You know you get in preparation mode, then you get into which includes starting with you what it is that you need to do. And then after you have started things are going as well as smooth as possible and you know you are living in the truth, you are living out your dream etc., then you get to relax and rest. That relaxation comes after you have accomplished it whether you succeed or not you get to relax knowing that you did at least do it. So, your relaxation is equivalent to being on vacation and returning home and just being able to rest. So, it goes preparation, work, relax in peace, rest again until you are ready to start again. So do not forget to have periods of resting and relaxation because the preparation and the work will probably be overwhelming at times but just know that you are resting, relaxation is the fruits of your labor. It comes after the fruits of your labor. After the preparation is the work mode the work mode is equivalent to the travel and getting to your destination in order for you to relax. And then returning home is being able to rest again.

Reflect

Think of yourself or your life as a research paper. You know some of the information from previous courses (life experiences), general knowledge (lessons) and re-searching (exploring). When it comes to your life, you may be confused about the directions to take. This can be from feeling afraid you do not know yourself well enough. Just know that you have all the information about yourself, abilities, and skills for your own re-search (self-analysis). Looking outside of yourself for answers may not be necessary because you have all the information needed to write a detailed and accurate re-search paper about yourself. The research paper can in-clude feedback, constructive criticism, and insight from others whether good or bad, but only you know the full details about yourself. You completed the studies, work, and research. You have all that knowledge and wealth of knowledge within you already. Remember you know you the best, yet there are times where we may need to look outside ourselves for additional resources and information to help us better understand and gain that clarity that we need. After you write your research paper, there is editing and revising. That would be you editing and revision in your life to make it better in which you can present it and resubmit it with a fresh start. Again, life does not come with a grade, only you put that restriction and limitation on yourself. Of course, everybody wants to get an A for their hard work, but the point is that you have made the effort, put in the work, did it to the best of your abilities, made alterations/revisions when and where needed. Just like a research paper sometimes there is more information needed. Analyzing what you have accomplished so far and what you want to accomplish affords you the capability to make a cohesive analysis. Fine tune the research of yourself to make it the best project you have ever completed.

Reflect

When you have been begging and crying or praying for change in your life, God/higher power puts things in front of you to start it. If you do not take heed, life becomes uncomfortable for you. The discomfort comes from something that you wanted, needed, and ask for but not acting toward. Life will throw hard balls at you to make you see the changes you need to make. The longer it takes for you to start moving, the more challenging and uncomfortable you feel. We might ignore the first two signs with little consequences, but the third, fourth, etc., time is when you will feel it. When you begin to trust yourself, you trust your higher power. Trust the discomfort, it is a learning experience. I have had the pleasure (not) of being uncomfortable in life. I had a few opportunities to relocate for a better life. Fear of the unknown prevented me from going. All the while, I was pleading for a change, depressed, and in a dark place. I am sure God had enough of me and my hardhead, so I have a soft ass. I hated every job and could not maintain one. I was ready to give up because I was out of options. I was fired from a job I HATED, had no more savings (thanks to the pandemic), and no other options for employment. That was when I packed what I could and blessed someone else with what I had (damn near everything). I had to start from scratch humbly because I ignored the signs. Oh, I still hate my job, but I wrote this book as a start to a new chapter in life. What are you begging God/spirit for? You aspire for more, but after work you are depleted of energy due to time spent working a job you hate. It is time for a change. That job is not going to fulfill you, but will provide necessary survival tools or resources. Change the mindset, especially if you are unable to find a job you enjoy. Even though you hate your job, consider it your side hustle. You may spend more time at the job opposed to your dream, but the job is funding your dream. The life you desire is to travel more. Your place of employment is the hustle to your dream. Be more passionate about your dream and let that job just be something on the side that comes with benefits. Do not let it stress you out.

Reflect

What holds a lot of people back from going toward their dreams is fear of success. For some, that fear and apprehension comes from not seeing other people do it and knowing that you will be the first to do it. That fear can deter you from going forth, but it can also be the driving force to get you going. You know that fear of being successful and accomplished is something that you never thought you could do. So, it feels like you are going out of the norm, you are defying the norms that was placed upon you by society. You may feel like an outcast or you may feel like you will not succeed because you feel like you do not have what it takes to do it. Your dreams are something that is beyond your wildest imagination. You may have an idea of it but you never really know what else comes with it. And other things that comes with it are not bad things. They are great things and the greatness is what scares you. So, the longer that you sit in this the longer you will feel uncomfortable, the longer you will feel incomplete. The fear that you may have could be seeing other people going for their dreams but being unsuccessful. That may not be your life because they may not have that drive, motivation, or that blessing you may have so do not go based off what you have seen or have not seen. Go based on your faith, go based on yourself. That is when you have to become your biggest supporter and it is hard when you don't have that encouragement to go forth and you have to utilize or use within you to go forth and at times it just that fire again goes down because you don't have that support around you. You may also see people who go for their dreams and they just seem so easy without any complications or roadblocks. But you never know what these people truly went through, the process that it took, or anything like that. You may only see the good, not everybody announces the bad because they want to seem successful. So, think of it like this, maybe you are going through the challenging times now, but the success is there once you start going forward toward your dreams.

Reflect

Sometimes it is hard for us to stay motivated when the world around us is so loud. That is when we take measures to quiet the world, our mind, and distractions. Taking a detour can be used to see the future ahead. It does not mean you are not going to get to that destination, it just means you are going a different route than anticipated. This is another avenue to find your muse to motivation. That detour may be required because that path you were taking was congested. How to generate this? Through reclusion, isolation, or remove ourselves from certain situations and people. We become motivated when we can see and think clearly. So, when you remove that noise and distraction from around the road ahead looks promising.

Reflect

_____

_____

_____

_____

_____

_____

_____

_____

_____

_____

_____

_____

_____

_____

_____

_____

Do not fret about your prayers not being answered right away. God/higher source/your higher self needs to heal you. When we think of healing, we think of just understanding and processing past traumas, relationships, etc. Some of the blessings or things that we ask for we need time to heal our heart. It is easier to heal yourself from the toxic and unhealthy things, but healing your heart is a different obstacle. It requires you to accept yourself, be gentle, and truly bask in the good and ugly parts of your essence. Having a heavy heart will not afford you the opportunity to truly relish in the blessing. It will take strength and courage to heal your heart and release what is holding you back. For instance, you cannot go into a new relationship, marriage, or parenthood with a heavy heart because it will linger. You are going to continue to struggle and possibly jeopardize it, although you have been blessed. Before you give up and feel your prayers are not being heard, heal yourself and mend that broken heart.

Reflect

Invest in yourself, so you can invest in your future. Say you want to start a business, but you are apprehensive because you do not feel like you have everything you need to start, such as the degree or certification. Yet, you have the experience and passion, that is something a formal education or training cannot provide. When you are thinking about that business plan or dream, do not forget to include your life's experiences in your skillset or abilities. If starting a food business is your dream, but you lack educational requirements, use what you have. You may have to go to culinary school, but you will go in with experience. So, for instance let us say you want to start a restaurant, but you did not go to school for business or culinary arts. Another option could be to start a side hustle of selling plates. Make do with what you have by making progress toward your dream. If being a life coach is a dream of yours then think about the qualities you already possess. Is it passion for helping and working with others while maintaining a nonjudgmental and safe environment from a sympathetic and empathetic approach? Then you might be on to something. You will need to do the research to find out how to live out your dream career. Hell, even those that desire to live a rich and abundant life and not having to work for someone else starts by figuring out how to achieve it. Your dream may be to find a wealthy spouse, so you will need to do the work to find out where to meet those individuals and how to maintain that lifestyle. The moral of the story is, when you want something in life, go for it. Do not let any blockages prevent you from pursuing it and be ready to put in the work to achieve it.

Reflect

Are you someone who is on social media and you may come across people who talk about manifesting and affirmations to change your life? When it comes to affirmations and manifestations each one is individualized just like your life is different from others and what works for one does not work for you, that means if you want to affirm yourself and manifest things into your life you do what meets your needs. So, your manifestation may come in a different form— whatever works for you. Your affirmations might be different than what others tell you that you need to say. When it comes to your life you do what works for you in the most healthy and positive way. Do not depend on others and do not go by what others may tell you that you need to do and it is the only way to do it because that is not true. Just like praying, you may pray differently or you may not go to church but that does not mean that you do not believe in God or a higher self. It means you do it in your own way and that does not make what you do and how you do it wrong. So, when we approach life, we have to approach it to what we have and know that we are able to do or if you're willing to challenge yourself to do it again that is individualized to you and your needs. For instance, you know people might tell you to love yourself daily while looking in the mirror. You may not feel attractive or think that you are attractive so saying that it will not make you want to do it or feel comfortable doing it. You might just tell yourself affirmations of things you like about yourself and skilled at doing. You, know again, whatever affirmations if that is what you want to do to inspire yourself then again modify it to work for you it does not have to be what others tell you to do because a lot of people just regurgitate and parrot information and it does not fit you. Just like all one size fits all is in all the time one size fits all sometimes it is one size fits most so again you have to do what works for you.

Reflect

The thing you mostly want in life whether it is to become a writer, a doctor, a life coach, to relocate, perfect relationship well at least perfect for you, may not be in the cards right now. What if that desire will cause you distractions? If you desire a new relationship, but the opportunity to excel in your career is the alternative, which one are you choosing? The relationship will come, but it will hinder you now if pursued. By removing the distraction, you can focus on your growth and what you need to in order to get to that next phase and living that dream life that you want and desire so badly. Growth does not stop once you have accomplished something. It continues now that you are in a different phase of the unknown, so you will be challenged to prosper and flourish.

Reflect

Exploring the world from a place of pain is different from exploring through growth and healing. Having a peace of mind and happiness hits different when you experienced the pain of suffering internally and feeling stifled. Some people may feel peace and/or healing is boring. Why the boredom? The lifestyle changes you make may be boring compared to the life you lived before. It may be overwhelming for others because of the emotional wreck they have become. The real peace is not allowing yourself to constantly be in fight or flight mode. No longer being on alert and ready to attack like in survival mode is a blessing. Being able to peacefully rest and enjoy the little things in life is a big step in the healing journey. It is about maintaining yourself and not allowing others to alter your mood, thoughts, or behaviors. You do this by self-analyzing and reflection. Do

I need to entertain this? Does this deserve my energy? Probably not. Feeding into someone who does not have peace is only feeding their needs they have not yet come to terms with. It is giving into someone who needs you to energize them negatively, but how does that benefit you? It may feel great and appropriate to partake in low vibrational antics at the time, but you will notice how it effects your spirit. Your peace is your protection. It protects you from stupidity and negativity. It protects you from yourself. Why fuck up your healing for someone that is not healed or knows thyself? You are not bored or overwhelmed; you are healed or healing. You are experiencing a different version of you. This is a great period for you to reevaluate your life from a peaceful, rested stance that will allow you to grow and prosper. You may feel like nothing is changing, but it is. You are a different person mentally and emotionally. Being in fight or flight is like an addiction. You need that drama or trigger to feel alive. Being in peace and healed is recovery from that addiction, so your concept of life and yourself changes. Learn to embrace and accept these changes. As any addict, you may relapse but when you are healed you are resilient and bounce right back. You may be mad at yourself, but do not be upset. You are human and life has its challenges. Being at peace and healed means you do not beat yourself up and love yourself through those relapses. It is time to change into the best version of yourself and only you can take credit for it. Why? Because you did the work. I am not saying you cannot or will not give credit to a higher power, but ultimately you did the work. Your God/source paved the way for you to get here, but it is up to you to do the hard and grueling footwork, not them. So do not look at it as boring, but as a rebirth—coming out of your cocoon, healing from your past, and going into the future in self-love, patience, and wisdom. Our children, friends, family, etc., need guidance and if we are always centered in anger, resentment, trauma, unbalance, etc., then who are the teachers? The ancestors? The knowledgeable ones? Allow yourself to be your teacher or the wise one. You know from firsthand experience of what needs to be changed and why. This may seem like a difficult feat if you allow yourself to believe it. You are the source of your life, so take control and revel in it. This is the era of your life that you are in control of, something you probably have not experienced before. It may be scary to have faith in yourself, but it is necessary to ascend.

Reflect

A man being more in love with you than you are with him means his love is keeping your dynamics strong. His love is strong enough to get you through tough times. Your love is strong enough to build him back up stronger when he is going through it. You loving him less does not equate to you not loving him at all, it just means you will provide necessary love when your time comes and his love is leading you. Not controlling, but leading you. His love allows you to be the great and amazing woman you are and an exceptional spouse. When you have to lead, he will follow, as you will with him. You are one another's energy. You are one another's love. This love is real. This love is cherished. This love is true. This love allows you to be feminine and him masculine.

Reflect

_____

_____

_____

_____

_____

_____

_____

_____

_____

_____

_____

_____

_____

_____

_____

_____

The devil is not always in the biblical sense of that entity who is out to destroy you. The devil comes in a form of family, friends, coworkers, etc. Just like there are ripples and the tides in the water that you may believe is ahead although it is calm, walking in faith allows you to try to tread knowing you are in the right direction. Always remember that you are your strength. Always remember to have your best interest at heart even when others do not have it for you. You always have to believe in yourself even when others don't and again sometimes your strength comes from people places and things that you may not anticipate, thought about, or wanted. Yet, you still have to go forth even though you may feel that there are troubles ahead. Those troubles are just something that you may anticipate due to how your journey went thus far. The road ahead and that path has been untraveled by you so it is something that is new that you should appreciate, enjoy, and walk by faith in. There will always be adversities in life, but how you get through it depends on the faith you have in yourself and if you have a higher power depends on the faith you have within your higher power. Just keep going although the road may be scary because it is something unknown to you. The unknown will be scary. The unknown will be terrifying. But the unknown is something that you need to become comfortable with in order to get ahead and to accept with all your faith, which may be for some people hard to accept. Life is a bitch and it will continue to be but it is all about your perspective on things. Do not allow your current mind-set to be the falter of your future. Do not allow others' mind-set and perspective of your life, which they have no experience of with your specific life, be the end all to you. Others may have a say in your life, your future, and your circumstances, but it is only from a tunnel vision perspective. Their mind-set and their perspective only derive from what they know but not what you know. You know more about you than anyone else will, so it is up to you to learn as much about yourself as you can to not allow others to change your perspective about yourself and the path you are going on.

Reflect

The mastery of turning your pain into power starts with changing your perception with an uncomfortable self-perspective. This is the beginning of a new season of your live once you embrace it. So be uncomfortably comfortable with evolving with each season of your life.

Reflect

When you do not have a healthy relationship with yourself, you will not have one with others. You may try to escape through others, but that can become toxic. You may start to rely on others to fix what you are refusing to. I learned I have been codependent on people mentally. My codependency resulted from people not staying around in my life long, so I knew not to get attached to them physically. I did not expect them to be supportive or form any true healthy relationship. My codependency or attachment to them was my expectations, the what ifs, and fantasies I have had of our relationship whether it was platonic or intimate. My codependency was rooted in an unrealistic attachment to those I had no business being attached to. It took a long time to see this, and once I did, I understood the types of relationships I had with others and why.

If codependency is an issue for you, start by assessing what you depend on others for. Yes, you do have needs, but sometimes we depend on others due to insecurity, fear, or other unhealed wounds. Take a step back and figure out your unhealthy attachment as it can lead to detrimental relationships with yourself and others.

Reflect

_____

_____

_____

_____

_____

_____

_____

_____

_____

_____

_____

_____

_____

_____

_____

_____

_____

_____

When you elevate and start to change your perspective/
outlook on life, you will be tested in areas to see how
much you have changed. For instance, if you have only
dealt with a certain type of person and relationships
because you felt that was all that you were worth, you
are now going to be tested with the same type of individuals to see if you have changed. So, let us say that
you were working on and changing your outlook on
relationships, love, your worth, the type of people that
you deal with intimately, those past people will come
into your life to see if you will give in to those old ways.
So, the test is to help you see how you have grown and
for you to make the decision whether it is worth it or
not. The test of whatever situation you have in life you
keep repeating is going to or may produce vulnerabil-
ity, desperation, a sense of insecurity to make you see

whether you are strong enough to go to the next level or not. Every time you go back to that same person, same types of people, or same types of situations, you will have to restart the cycle over and continue to learn more within that lesson because there is something that you are missing out on. You are not fully getting that lesson in its entirety. So, when that lesson does end or you have realized that growth, it may take some time for that product that you want or relationship or whatever you wanted to come into fruition. You must be patient with yourself, life, and God. Be patient with the process and do not rush because rushing it does not allow it to come into the beauty it can be.

Reflect

_____

_____

_____

_____

_____

_____

_____

_____

_____

_____

_____

_____

_____

_____

_____

_____

_____

_____

Turning your pain into power is for those who experience pain. For those who have had a very deep
connection and experience with pain. The pain can
be from a traumatic event, divorce, death of a loved
one, being fired, feeling lost, you know whatever
the pain is to you because it is your story. Pain can
also come from never going toward that life that you
wanted. Whether it be a school that you wanted to
attend, a job or career you wanted to go for, moving
somewhere— you know that pain of sitting back and
realizing you could be living a different life but something prevented you from fulfilling that path and now
you sit back in that pain and want to do something
different. So, I honestly wrote this book for myself
as I turned my pain into my power and it's not even
about the words that's in this book but the actions I

took toward writing this book. Hopefully, this book resonates with those who want to turn their pain into power.

Reflect

As your pain turns into power, you begin to reclaim yourself and the control you possess. Life seems simpler and flows with ease. You begin to trust and listen to yourself. You crave and desire change— change of how you present yourself, react, and think. You have more faith in God and yourself. You worry less, overthink less, not as angry, depressed, hopeless, confused, or lost. You have a sense of being. You feel whole and ready to embark on this journey we call life.

Reflect

Feeling incomplete in life because you lack certain things or experiences can be due to living in the past or future. Living in the past can make you feel incomplete about situations that did not occur or you should have done. Living in the future can make you feel incomplete because you currently do not have what it is you want or you are not where you want to be in life. Completeness comes with living in the present and honoring what you have accomplished, your growth, etc. Feeling incomplete can be motivation to focus on your goals and yourself for fulfillment.

Reflect

Rushing can make you miss out on important things such as enjoying the moment. Let's say you're moving into a new apartment or a new city. Yes, you are excited, anxious, planning, and rushing to get things in order. Have you taken the time to truly cherish the moment and check in with yourself? Or are you letting the experience, experience you? Although sometimes you may need to rush due to circumstances but allow yourself to reflect and rest after a major milestone/experience.

Reflect

Your overthinking can be a factor why you cannot enjoy certain things. You may internally prevent yourself from doing something because you will not enjoy it. For example, you want to work out but you will not start until you stop over analyzing and look at it as something positive/fun. You will not enjoy dating if you go into or see every date as a serial killer, liar, cheater, etc. So, changing your perception by taking control of your thoughts can allow you the freedom to align from a softer realm.

Reflect

Fear of change can hold you back. For instance, while growing up you know life and circumstances might have been different for the older generation but has changed drastically for us. For example, when you were younger if you were born in the 80s. During that time rent was cheaper, there were more jobs, the economy was more stable than what it is now, gas was cheaper, food was cheaper, and people interacted more. But now as you are an adult gas is extremely high, rent is unaffordable, jobs do not pay much, nobody wants to socialize or interact, so this change may be a difficult concept for some to grasp. With that being said, you have to allow yourself to adapt to these changes because expecting things to remain the same will only keep you stunted in where you are in life. So, in order to grow you need to be able to face that fear or look past those expectations and move forward with confidence.

Reflect

Be prepared to be tested on the journey to self-love. These tests are to help you see where you have excelled and evolved at and where you need to focus your attention. Some tests will be big, some will be small. You may be evaluated on your attitude. Are you still rude or have you changed into a more welcoming individual? Are you still aggressive or have softened up some? Do you still give your heart away easily or are you more guarded with discernment? Are you still easily manipulated and naïve or have you learned to see people and things for what they are? The lessons depend on you and your experiences. These tests help you determine if you are ready for the next chapter and this will require you to be vulnerable and honest. Did you learn the lesson or do you need to reread the chapter again because you missed something? Remember, we cannot go to the next chapter by failing the test. Take in the lesson you have learned to avoid repeating it. You must be patient with yourself and the process. Do not rush because it does not allow it to come into the beautifulness that it can be.

Reflect

Learning your value during a self-love journey is vital, yet confusing. When you do not see, know, or understand your value you settle for any and everything. Knowing your value and worth helps you establish boundaries. You notice and understand what does not serve your best interest. This allows you to make better decisions about the people, place, and things you engage in/with because you know your worth. You may want to partake in behaviors or activities that were once "fun or entertaining " but now you see how it is not. Settling for relationships, jobs, etc., will no longer be an option as it does not serve your highest good. So be gentle and patient with yourself as you come to terms with this.

Reflect

Surround yourself with people that cherish grow and new opportunities to expand in life. Some of us are or were magnetized toward unsavory people who have chaos in their lives, that is/was destructive to your well-being. These individuals are more than likely un-healed and stuck in their ways that is unproductive. This occurs when you, too, are chaotic mentally and emotionally to see the effects of having these types of individuals in your circle. Releasing that hold onto the dependence of chaos will allow you to free yourself from a world of turmoil and people that cater to mess.

Reflect

For the ladies, are you in your soft girl era? If not, why not? Being in your soft girl era is new for many of us as we have not learned to be soft, or always had/have to be tough and strong. That shit is tiring as you get older. Many people have opinions of what being in your soft era means, but this is for you to design. It does not always constitute material items, but it is a way of living. The soft era can be learning to take it slow in life and not rushing. It can be resting and relaxing without guilt. Working on personal development such as reading, getting physically fit, taking more stride in your appearance, saying no, and being taken care of by someone instead of taking on the load all the time.

Reflect

If insecurity or low self-esteem is your pain, that is okay. You will not be everyone's cup of tea, and believe me, you do not want to be. As you embark on your self-love journey to confidence it will be challenging. You may start to evolve and experiment with new hairstyles, wardrobe, etc. as you develop a new sense of self. At times, your old self may reappear and try to diminish what you have accomplished. Those negative thoughts or views of yourself may emerge despite the changes you have made. If you lost weight, your old self may say you are still fat. Your old self may call you ugly, even if you changed those things that made you feel unattractive. During your evolution, that pain morphs into power and you will see glimpses of the new you. The beautiful and sexy new you. That power has allowed you to become more confident as you deplete those negative images of yourself, those insecurities, the pain, and the past. This new you will want to be the only perception you have of yourself. You will not want to look like what you have been through but who you are becoming on your self-love journey. Remember, do not seek validation from others on the new you. Be your own validation and praise yourself because you are doing GREAT.

Reflect

Many of the unfortunate obstacles we endure in life is to strengthen us and make us more resilient. It is hard to understand that during those times, but once you have connected with yourself, you may understand it. For some, it has pushed us to where we want and need to be. If you lost your job and is struggling from that, you could strengthen yourself to do something better. If you continue to take jobs that are not aligned with you then you will continue to experience the same outcome. Maybe it is time for a change. This applies to other circumstances. You will develop the ability to bounce back and go for what you want by being resilient. You will decrease your self-pity with the strength to want more for yourself.

Reflect

Something important to keep in mind during your self-love journey and just in life is you do not owe anyone anything. No one owes you anything. So, let's say you become successful in your own right, this can be financially. You know you may have family, friends, or whoever feeling like you owe them. Now, if you owe them money for you know something that you borrow you know what you should pay them back. But if you have accomplished your success by yourself, you don't owe anyone anything. So also take note is that you do not need to be apologetic for who you are and what you have become. Except if you are a piece of s*** then maybe you do need to be apologetic. You know during your self-love journey and being connected to yourself; you may want to make amends with others and that is perfectly fine. You know that is for you to release and to move past so you can continue a fruitful life. Even after you make amends the other person may not be as receptive or open to it, but you did your part. They have to come to terms and grips with that and you know again you owe nobody nothing and they owe you nothing. Overall, you learn to be the best version of you for yourself and to avoid conflict with others in the future OR to be able to resolve those with openness and love.

Reflect

Part of your journey will be releasing anger. Anger toward your parents, children, exes, and friends. Your anger may be from feeling neglected by those you love and vice versa. Your job is to understand the anger and why you feel that way. Again, no one owes you anything. Not an apology or acknowledgement, so do not expect it. You can share your feelings, but others may have a different viewpoint of the situation. Release that pain and hurt accepting what did or did not happen, so you do not fester in that anger. Allowing the anger to have a vice grip on you keeps the pain and gives it fire to grow or simmer. By releasing it, you give yourself the freedom to move on and be at peace. You do not have to forgive or forget, that is your choice, but you should want to feel that weight lifted off your spirit and chest. It will not be easy, but you will feel a sense of relief from the burden.

Reflect

The saying that God gives his strongest battles to his toughest soldiers can be interpreted as you having the strength, and power to fight those battles you are enduring. God or spirit know your capabilities, so they give you those battles to help strengthen you and to move you forward. God/spirit cannot want it more than you do. It is possible those battles that you are experiencing is getting you to the next level that you prayed for. When you are in that battle, it is your job to understand the message and the plan that God/spirit has for you, as well as the plan that you have for yourself and how to come out victorious. For instance, you have a friend/family member/coworker etc., that continues to talk about something that they want. It could be buying a house, getting a new job, wanting to move, etc. If they are not doing the work, you cannot be the one that motivates or be the one to continue to validate them wanting whatever it is that they want. The battle is for them to conquer. Nothing in life comes easy, so those battles are to help you get through the process and come out with wisdom, knowledge— whatever. Your battles are meant for you to fight. It is not to say that you will not get assistance along the way, but you need to fight that battle. So, let's say that you get through the battle with codependency from others to help you because you are afraid to fight that battle. Did you actually win that battle? Are you able to say at the end that you actually won? No, because what did you learn? What did you gain? Nothing. The only thing that you've gained or learned is to continue to depend on people and not strengthen yourself. That is what those battles are for, to help you learn lessons and to appreciate the win. It is not your job to fight others' battles, as you will only take on obstacles that is not yours and create burdens on yourself. You can advise, but it is not your job to do the work of someone else. You do not like to do the work of your coworkers who get paid to do their job, so you do not want to fight a battle that is not meant for you to fight.

Reflect

_____

_____

_____

_____

_____

_____

_____

_____

_____

_____

_____

_____

_____

_____

_____

_____

_____

The self-love journey is not all peace and hair grease. It is a whole bald headed, snaggletooth, cockeyed, slew footed hoe. Do not expect your life or journey to be perfect once you are in it because you are still learning. If you master the perfection of healing, hey hats off to you and can you guide me to be like you. This journey is about obtaining wisdom and knowledge while learning, growing, and evolving. You will enter different seasons in life, which may be full of trials and tribulations or full of joy and excitement. The point is, regardless of the season, take each day at a time, conquer what needs to be conquered, and have fun when it is permitted. Most of all remain in a state of peace and be accepting of what is coming your way. Remember, you are not in competition and there is no deadline for this, so be easy and enjoy life the way YOU want to. Another part of the self-love and healing journey that may not be explained or discussed enough is that you are still human. Some people may learn to love themselves, but still cuss people out. Some are reformed and only center in light and love. Regardless of how you maneuver, the objective is to have self-love. Not every day will be all roses. You may still struggle as you continue to heal, but it will get better. Continue to be patient and enjoy the ride. I have heard some people say they will remain celibate during their healing, which I completely understand. But if you need to hunch on someone or need someone to hunch on you, please do you. Your needs will not stop because you are healing. The difference is your standards may change on those you choose to be intimate with. Again, do you, whether you choose to hunch or not.

Reflect

A part of being vulnerable with yourself is learning to be you when no one is around. Learning to relax, be goofy, and free. If we cannot be ourselves with ourselves, how can we be authentic around others? We cannot be afraid to let our guard down. This allows us to see who we truly are and learn to be us all the time. If you are scared to wear a bathing suit, start wearing one around the house. You may be comfortable doing so or you may be self-conscious even alone. You may have insecurities with your body, so get comfortable with seeing yourself in revealing clothing. Why go to the pool or beach and not have a good time because you feel insecure? You will never know how good the sun feels on your skin when sunbathing because of your fear. Learn to get comfortable in your uncomfortable moments. This apply to life. Why be uncomfortable because you cannot be yourself or in public? Being uncomfortable is the indicator of what you need to work on. If you are uncomfortable speaking in large crowds, wearing certain clothes, hairstyles, etc., then your assignment is to get comfortable in that environment. The moral of the story is fuck what you believe others may be thinking because most of the time that is your insecurities and internal Debbie Downer. There may be times when people say something. I am not condoning violence, but cuss them clean smooth out. It is none of their business. Your confidence is a threat and they are using whatever artillery they have to ease the threat they feel. This has nothing to do with you, and there is nothing wrong with expressing it. Be confident when you are most insecure as it is the time when you will need it most.

Reflect

_____

_____

_____

_____

_____

_____

_____

_____

_____

_____

_____

_____

_____

_____

_____

_____

While healing, you may start to think about the people, places, and things you have allowed in your life. As you continue to mend yourself, you may start to look at these things differently. You may start to analyze your relationships and ponder if you see a future with them. This pertains to all relationships. Can you see them as an asset in where you are going spiritually, mentally, emotionally, or financially? Or are they a liability that will hinder your growth? This apply to places and things. Your old self may have tolerated it, but the evolved you will oppose distractions. If you have friends that only want to party, smoke, drink, and chase after the next nut, does this align with your values? Does where you live stunt your growth? Maybe it is time for a change. Relocating can be the best decisions for those that can. That change of environment or pace can be that much needed push. It is okay to change your environment and rearrange your space (removing clutter) and you do not have to justify it. Are you concerned how the people in your life will react/respond? If they are a real one, they will understand and support your decision. If they do not, they removed themselves with their decision. Welcome change and know everything is flowing accordingly.

Reflect

How peaceful do you want your life to be? How healed do you want to be? Understanding this will provide the outline, blueprint, and manual to achieve the peace you require. You dictate and provide the instructions on your peace and healing. If you allow it to, this can be exhilarating. You may take more vacations or your first vacation, have solo time, get massages, date, whatever peace and healing means for you. For some, it can mean going to therapy/life coach, smiling and laughing more, drinking or smoking less, even going cold turkey from whatever addiction you may have. It is whatever that will encourage and enhance your healing, peace, and self-love. You illustrate and narrate this, which makes it more blissful, again if you allow it.

Reflect

Consistency and self-discipline is required to keep going. Understanding the barriers helps you navigate through what is hindering you. It is not that you cannot do it or lack the motivation, but accountability within yourself is stagnating your progress. Some things you want in life is also delayed because you are not ready. Any apprehension or uncertainty can delay it. The possibility of sabotaging can delay it. Make sure you know what you want and determine how much you want it. Do not be afraid to pursue your dreams, just make sure you are ready to put in the work and be prepared to sweat. You may sweat a little, you may sweat a lot, but you will sweat. Being certain about what you want to achieve makes the process worthwhile, so again ensure you are ready because it is time to put in the work.

Reflect

If you have come to the decision to withdraw from the dating scene and wait for the "one," it does not mean you are waiting for the perfect person. Of course no one is perfect, but you are waiting for someone you do not have to settle for or someone that has settled for you. During this time, you begin to enjoy life being single, which may be a new experience. It is not to say you will not die, but you will do so with clear judgment, discernment, and your intuition. As you heal and walk in self-love you will no longer be attracted to the same types of people as your motives and mindset has altered. When you are approached by what you settled for in the past, you will reject it. You are now able to discern who you will and will not entertain. When you do encounter what you desire, do not rush or expect the first one to be the one. Remember to stick to your values and your life's plans. If you meet a man that meets many of the characteristics you require, but he does not want children or wants to get married, and that is what you want, do not settle. If you are spiritual and again meet another amazing being, they require church involvement and that is not your lifestyle, do not settle. There is nothing wrong with not settling. Would you prefer to be single and dating or settling for someone you perceive as better than the past while unhappy and unfulfilled? The choice is yours to make, so make it a worthy decision. When you start to only date within your standards, you stop giving your time to trolls and fools. Just think back on the time, money, energy, your essence, blah blah you have spent on someone you knew was not worth your time. It became draining after a while. Now, you can preserve that for you and the right one. You do not want to be scared or afraid to put in effort with the right one because you have been depleted, so save it for someone that is worth it. Hell, if you do not find the one you still have yourself to give to.

When you are healing and coming into peace, it involves a lot of thinking and processing. Thinking and processing brings to light things that are not for you. You may start to analyze your situation and think of how it is unfulfilling, makes you unhappy, and realize change is needed. You may start to feel that you are complaining and is ungrateful about your situation. It is not being ungrateful, you are just processing and understanding what needs to change. Thinking and processing allows you to assess the circumstances and come up with a game plan on how to move forward. Do not feel guilty for wanting more and better for yourself. Feelings of guilt can result in overthinking and talking yourself out of what you want. That overthinking can be equivalent to a hater. Do not be your own Debbie Downer. Uplift yourself and know you deserve it. Procrastinating can come from the inner hater and delay your happiness. You can be your own worst enemy in terms of thinking so process, understand, and get going toward your success.

Reflect

Creating a happy place for you can also be beneficial while you are healing. A happy place does not mean spending a bunch of money, but creating a space that is for you to relax and just be calm. I understand that in our financial times some may not have money to splurge, so work with what you have. This can include rearranging furniture in your living room, bedroom, or whatever space is in your house that will be your temple of peace. Your happy place can be taking a candle lit bath while relaxing and just having that time for you. Your happy place can be becoming a plant parent— add plants to your space and watch them thrive. It could be coloring, crafting, or taking up a hobby. Your happy place is whatever brings you peace and allows you to shut your mind off. It does not have to be meditation because it is not for everyone. Your happy place is meant just for you and only you. This is a place where no one can disturb or affect you. Also, do not be afraid to splurge on yourself. This does not mean to live beyond your means or spend what you do not have, but do not be afraid to treat yourself. You do not work just to pay bills because all your money will more than likely always go to bills. Treat yourself, do not feel guilty about it, and do not try to rationalize it. By rationalizing you needing rest, a new outfit, a new perfume, some new curtains, or whatever it is that you want means that you are not putting yourself first. Then that means you need to justify treating yourself. It is not just treating yourself, but taking care of you and doing what makes you happy. Some may struggle with doing things or buying things for themselves, but always buy and treat other people. This does not just include children, family, spouse, or friends it just means anybody in general you are always doing something for. If you are the type of person who rarely has anyone do things for you on the whim, do it for yourself. As you start to put yourself first and spoil yourself, you may start to attract people or accept others treating you without guilt or feeling obligated to return the favor.

Reflect

It is also important to take time for yourself and not feel guilty about it. Having more time can be meal prepping, do chores early, etc., so you have more time to yourself. When you are making more time for yourself, it is not being lazy. Some people may feel that they are being lazy, not being productive, or getting things done. But how can you be productive when you are tired, stressed, and overwhelmed all the time? You are not being lazy you are resting, which is more than likely needed. Take time to relax to get your mind, body, and spirit aligned so you can put your best foot forward. Do not work off the adrenaline of stress because you will quickly burn out. Even if it is for a few minutes, hours a day, or week— take that time for yourself. Do not run yourself ragged. Some people sit in their cars before going in the house after work or a long day. If that is your time then let it be without the guilt. You do not have to justify or explain yourself; you just have to be in your zone. The objective is to be in tune with yourself in calmness. For those that have kids or take care of others, this is very important to establish. You can get burned out quickly. Always on the go and no time to be still can wreak havoc on you mentally. Do not let your bedtime be the only time you take a break because your sleep can be affected. You will not be fully rested or refreshed in the morning. This is coming from personal experience. I took care of an ill parent that was in and out of the hospital while working part-time, getting a graduate degree, and going to the gym regularly. The gym helped tremendously, but I was exhausted. It took years to no longer feel burned out. Life does not stop for anyone, so make life slow down and you catch up while you get yourself together. My grades, mom, and work needed me, but I also needed me. Unfortunately, the pandemic happened, my mom passed, but I still had school and work. Both were affected and so was I. God finally answered my prayers as he made me stronger and able for the next path. The path was relocating with family who were loving and supportive. I still struggled internally, but I was able to push through after more lessons. Lessons in love, life, and myself. This is how this book came to be. I was able to be still. I thought I was in control of the timeline of being still, but I was sadly mistaken. The reflections of this book came from my peace when I learned those hard and grueling lessons. I am still learning, but I am more receptive to those lessons and my life has improved. I am far from perfect; however, I am better than what I was a few years ago. When you start to process things, you find out how much there is to unpack. It is not an easy feat as you may not want to accept it. Acceptance is the easy part. Learning and evolving from it is the hard part as you will shed parts of yourself and be vulnerable with what you have experienced. Take it easy is the best advice I can give because it will be hard for some, if not most.

Reflect

Grief does not only come when someone passes away. Grief is when you see situations for what it is. Grief comes in many stages, and it is not linear. Sometimes you are angry, then accept the situation, then angry again. This can come about when you are shedding parts of yourself that has gotten you through life. You may grieve relationships, yourself, or whatever you have to let go of. At times, you may be unable to cope with what you are feeling and experiencing. It can feel like a death, but there can be a rebirth. A rebirth to a fresh start. A rebirth of a new you. It may feel like there is no end, but that is only if you choose to believe it. Take your time to go through the phases, regardless of how long or how many of the phases you repeat. It is a purging. It is not comfortable, but you can learn to adapt and be at peace with that loss. That loss does not mean the end, it just means an end to that loss. Ask yourself why you want or need to let go. This may help you through the process, especially if it is something that brings hurt and pain. Let it go. Mourn, grieve, have a mental funeral, but let it go so you can heal.

Reflect

Hopefully, after you read this book you have under-stood, acknowledged, accepted, and embraced your pain. What do you do now? It's the fun part now. This is your era of self-love. You are triumphing toward great-ness. You are at PEACE. You are HEALED (possibly more in some areas than others). You know how to better manage/deter from pain. You are LIVING life for YOU. You are no longer pondering on what to do because you are doing it. You are taking chances. You are no longer scared. You are no longer afraid to shine and be your authentic self. You are surrounding your-self with others that align with you. You have a sense of FREEDOM you did not possess before; freedom to be free. You have a more optimistic and realistic outlook on yourself and the life you desire. You look at yourself more each day with admiration You move at your own pace and strive to be a better you all the time. Most of all, you are NO LONGER IN PAIN. This is the era where you dictate your life. In the past, the pain dictated and controlled you. You are now healed and minding your peace, so stay peaceful, wise, and internally abundant while you honor thyself on the next blissful chapter of blessings.

Reflect

Be submissive to the self-love journey. Being submissive of healing is to stop resisting change that will naturally occur. Healing is about empowerment. It is learning to listen to yourself and going with the flow it brings. The flow of direction down a new path. Being submissive comes with surprises. Surprises of insight to the dilemmas and seeing the greatness in them. It is about resilience and recognizing your strength. It is overcoming obstacles and becoming a better person from them. Being submissive wants you to stop holding yourself back in life. Relinquish control and trust the process. Have faith that everything for you will fall into place. Have faith in yourself and stop doubting. A key factor when healing is to take breaks. Every day you do not need to work on yourself. Some days you just need to relax and let loose. Shit, you may not want to or need to do anything but sleep, watch television, eat, or do the nasty. Taking a break will not halt your process or progress. Taking a break affords you the ability to live life. It can energize you and potentially help your healing process. Feeling the need to always work on self-development and growth can become overwhelming, so that is your sign to take it easy. Just like work, you need a break from working and have time to yourself. Do not treat your healing journey like a job as it may start to feel like one. Enjoy life and live a little. Go on vacation, take a day trip, go to the spa. Do something to get your mind off it and do not worry about it. Return where you left off when you are ready. As your pain turns into power, you begin to reclaim it. Life seems simpler and flows with ease. You begin to trust and listen to yourself. You crave and desire change. Change of how you present yourself, react, and think. You have more faith in God and yourself. You worry less, overthink less, not as angry, depressed, hopeless, confused, or lost. You have a sense of being. You feel whole and ready to embark on this journey we call life.

Reflect

Note from Author

Do not fear change or growth, as it will be critical in your development of self. Take control of your life and marvel in the unknown as you explore the pain and healed version of yourself.

Reflective Questions

1. What is your pain, and where did it derive from?

2. How have you given your power away (mentally, emotionally, financially, spiritually, physically, energetically)?

3. How have you been managing/coping with your pain?

4. What is your definition of self-love?

5. Do you love yourself, why or why not?

6. How do you plan to take your power back?

7. What are your goals and dreams? What is stopping you from achieving them?

Your Reflections

www.ingramcontent.com/pod-product-compliance
Lightning Source LLC
Chambersburg PA
CBHW020439130626
46549CB00001B/209